The DRED SCOTT CASE

TESTING THE RIGHT TO LIVE FREE

JENNIFER FLEISCHNER

Spotlight on American History
The Millbrook Press • Brookfield, Connecticut

Cover photographs courtesy of The Granger Collection.

Photographs courtesy of North Wind Picture Archives: pp. 12, 17, 22-23, 33, 34; Scala Art Resources, NY: p. 15; The Granger Collection: p. 25 (both); Corbis-Bettmann: pp. 39, 42, 46, 48; Missouri Historical Society, St. Louis: pp. 52 (Tiffany Collection), 54-55; Map by Joe LeMonnier.

Library of Congress Cataloging-in-Publication Data
Fleischner, Jennifer.
The Dred Scott case : testing the right to live free /
by Jennifer Fleischner.
p.   cm. — (Spotlight on American history)
Includes bibliographical references and index.
ISBN 0-7613-0005-8 (lib. bdg.)
1. Scott, Dred, 1809–1858—Trials, litigation, etc.—Juvenile
literature.   2. Slavery—Law and legislation—United States—
Juvenile literature.   3. Slavery—United States—Legal status of
slaves in free states—History. I. Title. II. Series.
KF228.S27F57   1996
342.73′087—dc20   [347.30287]   96-17034   CIP

Published by The Millbrook Press, Inc.
2 Old New Milford Road, Brookfield, Connecticut 06804

Contents

The DRED SCOTT CASE

Introduction

A WAR OF WORDS

At eleven o'clock, March 6, 1857, the old courtroom on the ground floor of the Capitol was filled to overflowing with lawyers, reporters, and curious spectators. It was a plain, medium-sized room, with a vaulted ceiling supported by columns. Windows lined the wall behind a row of nine seats that waited empty at the front of the room. The crowd buzzed with excitement, eager and expectant. Suddenly, a hush fell over the room.

The nine Supreme Court judges, in black silk robes, filed silently into the courtroom. They moved slowly toward the vacant seats beneath the windows. At the head of the procession was a tall, thin man, with a pale, homely, and careworn face. He was stooped slightly from age, though he walked with a firm step. "That's Taney," a round of whispers circulated through the room. Others whispered that the judge was about to turn eighty.

Chief Justice Roger Brooke Taney took his place at the center of the bench. The other eight justices settled themselves around him. The light from the windows behind the judges shone into

[7]

the audience, and many in the crowd could not see the nine justices' faces. Taney took up the papers before him and began to read. He was clearly exhausted. His hands trembled, and his voice, low from the start, became weaker and weaker, gradually making it difficult to hear him.

It took Justice Taney two hours to deliver his historic 1857 decision in the case of *Dred Scott* v. *John F. A. Sanford*. His was to be the final legal ruling on the lawsuits that had begun in 1846 in St. Louis, Missouri, when a slave known as Dred Scott sued his master for his and his family's freedom. In his suit, Scott claimed that he, his wife, and daughters were entitled to their freedom since their master had taken them to live for a period of time in free territory, where slavery was prohibited. Scott's suit also declared that he was a citizen of Missouri and that he and his family were being held illegally as slaves.

It had been eleven years from the day that Dred Scott began his legal ordeal in a St. Louis courthouse to this morning in March 1857, when the Supreme Court made its final ruling on his case. By the time Justice Taney delivered the Court's opinion, the issues involved went far beyond the important but relatively narrow question of the Scott family's personal freedom. Dred Scott's lawsuit had moved to the center of the nation's conflict over slavery. The people crammed into that Washington, D.C., basement courtroom were there to hear Justice Taney address these larger political concerns.

The nation was bitterly divided over the questions before the Supreme Court that day. Were African Americans citizens of the United States, and therefore entitled to bring lawsuits before a federal court? Did Congress have the constitutional power to prohibit slavery in the western territories? Could Congress interfere with a slaveholder's ownership of his property, including his slaves? What were the rights of slaves brought to live in free states, where the laws against slaveholding contradicted those of slave states?

When the day was over, the words that Chief Justice Taney spoke so softly resounded loudly throughout the land. They set off a war of words over slavery that many came to believe only a ferocious civil war could put to rest.

1 "Three fifths of all other Persons"

From the very beginning of European exploration in the New World, Africans came as explorers, servants, and slaves. In the fifteenth and sixteenth centuries, Africans arrived with the expeditions led by Spanish, Portuguese, and French explorers.

In 1619 the captain of a Dutch merchant ship unloaded twenty Africans at the British colony at Jamestown, Virginia. They were listed not as slaves but as indentured servants, who were required to work for their masters for a specified number of years.

But soon the Virginia colonists found that they were unable to clear the forests fast enough and grow as much tobacco as they wanted with only the labor of Indians and servants. They began to turn to the idea of holding African workers as slaves for life.

Several factors encouraged their thinking. Africans were not Christians and could not read or write English, and so many colonists considered them to be less than human. Because of their skin color, black slaves could not escape from their masters without being easily identified.

Slaves were captured and brought from Africa to America under conditions so brutal that almost half of the people died during the voyage. Those who survived were destined to a fate not much better.

There seemed to be an endless supply of Africans to be imported from Africa. Slavery spread through the colonies, and the colonists soon recognized the need for laws to regulate it. By the mid-1660s, slavery was officially recognized and protected in the laws of Virginia and Maryland. To ensure that there would always be slaves, laws were written so that black children born in the colonies would be slave or free depending upon the condition of the mother. The colonists' slave codes were modeled on Caribbean slave laws. Slaves could not leave their plantations without the written permission of their masters. Slaves found guilty of robbery were to receive sixty lashes and be placed in a pillory, where their ears were to be cut off. A slave could be whipped, branded, or maimed for insulting a white person or a free black.

Most of the slave codes were intended to make slaves dependent on their masters, so that they would not rebel or run away. Slave codes forbade slaves from learning to read or write, and some prohibited slave marriages. Slaves also could not own firearms or property, and they could not testify in a court of law against whites.

By the time Thomas Jefferson presented his Declaration of Independence to the Continental Congress in 1776, slavery was part of the American way of life. Slavery was legal throughout the colonies, in the South as well as in the North. But many colonists, Jefferson included, were troubled by slavery. How could they follow the Declaration's statement that "all men are created equal" and yet also support the holding of slaves?

The Founding Fathers were still struggling with the problem of slavery when they drafted the Constitution in 1787, the document upon which they built their new nation. Meanwhile, the rift between pro-slavery and anti-slavery people widened. The Revo-

SLAVE LIFE ON
THE PLANTATION

BY THE NINETEENTH CENTURY, many slaves lived on enormous plantations that ranged across the South. Field slaves labored in small groups under the control of a slave driver who was usually a slave himself. Women often worked in the main house as cooks, maids, and nurses for the master's and mistress's children. Slaves also worked as carpenters, blacksmiths, and coopers.

Before they were put to work themselves (girls as young as four or five years old baby-sat for infants), slave children were cared for in groups by older black women. Sometimes the mistress would help raise the slave children and nurse them when they were sick.

Slaves often lived with their families in rows of slave cabins. These had a dirt floor, one window, and an opening instead of a door. Slaves often slept on the ground on mattresses made of straw, grass, or hay.

Slave codes required masters to give their slaves a monthly allowance of food and a yearly supply of clothing. But slaves who could not find ways to get more food often went hungry. The men got two shirts, two pairs of trousers, and a pair of shoes each year. The women received one or two dresses. The children wore hand-me-downs or coarse linen shirts and no shoes or stockings.

Yet, out of these hardships, slaves created a rich culture of work songs and spirituals, quilts, dances, folktales, and social and religious beliefs and customs.

lutionary War had spread the belief in freedom from tyranny for all, and inspired the rise of an anti-slavery movement in the North, where several states moved to abolish slavery. Meanwhile, the South had become increasingly pro-slavery. By the 1790s, there were about 700,000 slaves in the United States. In 1793, Eli Whitney invented the cotton gin, which helped in the difficult task of seeding cotton. This increased the South's production of cotton, making the South heavily dependent upon slave labor for its economic success.

The framers of the Constitution debated how their document should deal with the matter of slavery. They avoided using the words "slavery" or "slave," but they clearly had slavery in mind in three specific clauses.

First, they argued about the representation of slaves in the Congress, and how slaves should be counted. As a compromise between the North and South, they decided to count free people as whole and "those bound to Service for a Term of Years . . . three fifths of all other Persons." Second, they agreed to the compromise to continue the slave trade for another twenty years, after which it would be abolished. Finally, they decided that people in free states must return runaway slaves to their masters, since the slaves shall not "in Consequence of any Law or Regulation . . . be discharged from such Service or Labour . . ." simply because they were on free soil. This was known as the fugitive slave clause.

Right up to the Civil War, anti-slavery and pro-slavery forces struggled furiously for control of the Congress and the federal government. Who controlled the government mostly depended upon who had the most votes in Congress—the Northern states where slavery had been abolished, or the Southern states where slavery was allowed.

Eli Whitney's cotton gin, which seeded raw cotton more easily and efficiently than by hand, made cotton growing a very profitable business. However, the cotton gin made the South even more dependent upon slave labor to clear the fields, farm, pick, and process the cotton.

In 1819, when settlers in Missouri applied for statehood, Congress began a two-year battle over the question of whether Missouri would be a slave or free state. (Missouri was part of a vast territory gained through the Louisiana Purchase of 1803.) Southerners argued that banning slavery from Missouri would deprive

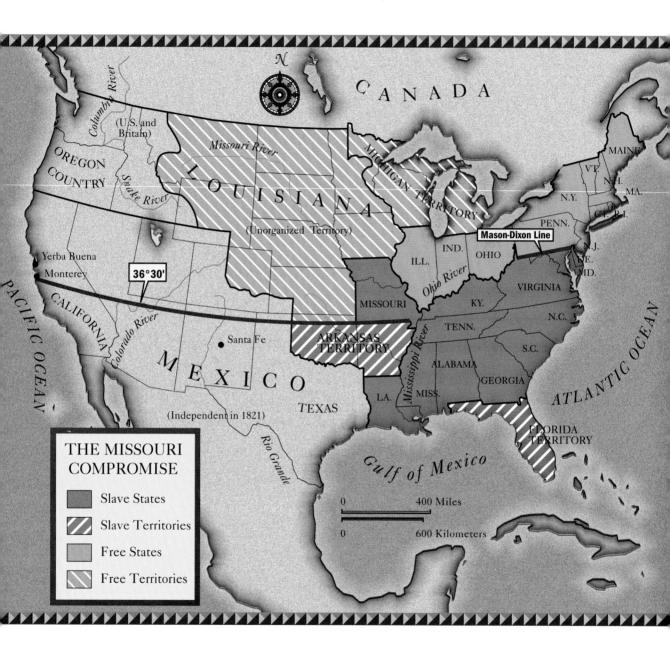

THE MISSOURI COMPROMISE

Slave States
Slave Territories
Free States
Free Territories

CANADA

OREGON COUNTRY
(U.S. and Britain)

Columbia River

Snake River

LOUISIANA

Missouri River

(Unorganized Territory)

MICHIGAN TERRITORY

MAINE
VT.
N.H.
N.Y.
MA.
CT.
PENN.
R.I.
N.J.
DE.
MD.

Mason-Dixon Line

IND.
OHIO

ILL.

Ohio River

MISSOURI

KY.

VIRGINIA

N.C.

36°30'

PACIFIC OCEAN

CALIFORNIA

Yerba Buena
Monterey

Colorado River

Santa Fe

MEXICO

(Independent in 1821)

Rio Grande

TEXAS

ARKANSAS TERRITORY

Mississippi River

TENN.

S.C.

ALABAMA

GEORGIA

MISS.

LA.

ATLANTIC OCEAN

FLORIDA TERRITORY

Gulf of Mexico

0   400 Miles

0   600 Kilometers

them of their property—that is, their slaves. But Northerners did not want slavery to spread. By 1820, Maine also sought to join the Union, and this set the stage for a compromise: Missouri would be admitted as a slave state, while Maine would be a free state. Also, slavery would be banned in the rest of the Louisiana Territory north of latitude 36°30′.

Known as the Missouri Compromise of 1820, this law was in force when Dred Scott, a Missouri slave, was taken by his master across this dividing line—into territory where slavery had been excluded—to live as a slave on free soil.

The Missouri Compromise was a political trade-off. Missouri was allowed to be admitted to the Union as a slave state and Maine as a free state. This kept a balance within the union.

2

A Slave Called Dred Scott

The slave who became known as Dred Scott was most likely born in Virginia around 1795. We do not know his exact birthdate: slave births were simply recorded by their masters, along with their lists of other property, such as horses, mules, and goats. In fact, to learn about Dred Scott's early years, we have to look to his master, Peter Blow.

In 1819, the year before the Missouri Compromise, Peter Blow owned 860 acres (348 hectares) in Southampton County, Virginia. But the land was worn out from years of cultivation, and Blow was unable to support his family—his wife, Elizabeth, and their seven children. Like many Easterners in his day, Peter Blow decided to move west, in search of a better life. He eventually settled, in 1830, in St. Louis, Missouri, at the junction of the Missouri and Mississippi rivers, the gateway to the West. It was here, also, that North met South, at the border between the slave states and free soil.

St. Louis in 1830 was a bustling frontier town. Steamboats ran up and down the Mississippi River, connecting St. Louis to New Orleans. St. Louis was a slaveholding town whose masters had fought hard to make sure that Missouri was a slave state. But it was also home to many Northerners, who had come soon after the Louisiana Purchase in 1803. Here, the Blows opened a boarding-house, known as the Jefferson Hotel, in a large house that they rented for $25 a month.

In addition to his family, Peter Blow also brought six slaves to St. Louis with him. One of them was a short, stocky man who seems to have been named Sam. Sam had very dark skin and was probably only about 5 feet (150 centimeters) tall. Blow could not use Sam in his boardinghouse, so he hired him out, and Sam worked for the next year or two as a deckhand on the riverboats that went up and down the Mississippi. Sam could neither read nor write, and when he later became famous as Dred Scott, he signed the legal documents with his "mark" instead of a signature.

A year after the Blows had moved to St. Louis, Elizabeth Blow died. Blow gave up the hotel business and moved his family to another house early in 1832. But he soon fell sick, and died in June. The family sold Sam to Dr. John Emerson for $500, to pay off some of Peter Blow's debts.

Very little evidence exists to tell us how Dred Scott felt about being sold. There is a story that when he learned he had been sold, he ran away to hide in a nearby swamp. Yet another story has it that he begged Emerson to buy him after being whipped by Peter Blow. We also do not know when he began using the name Dred Scott, although it seems to have been during the time he was owned by Emerson.

Peter Blow could not use Sam (Dred Scott) in his boarding house, so Sam was hired out to work as a deckhand on the riverboats that traveled the Mississippi.

Finally, we know little about Dred Scott's character. He was remembered by a onetime governor of Missouri as being "very much respected." A St. Louis newspaperman who interviewed Scott in 1857 said that he was "illiterate but not ignorant," with a "strong common sense." But accounts of his personal life remain vague. What we do know, however, is where Dred Scott traveled and lived as the slave of Dr. Emerson.

When Dred Scott sued his master for his freedom, he claimed that he was entitled to be free because he had lived for a time with his master in free territory, where slavery was forbidden. This happened when he was Dr. Emerson's slave.

Emerson, a graduate of the University of Pennsylvania, was living in St. Louis when he purchased Dred Scott. But he was hoping to receive a commission as an assistant surgeon in the United States Army. In 1833, Emerson's appointment came through, and he was ordered to report immediately to Fort Armstrong in Illinois. When he traveled North, he took his recently bought slave with him. Thus, Scott went with his master to live in a free state.

In 1836 the Army decided to abandon Fort Armstrong, and Emerson was transferred to Fort Snelling, on the west bank of the Mississippi near what would become St. Paul, Minnesota. This was part of the Wisconsin Territory until 1838, when it was shifted to the Iowa Territory. The whole area lay within the boundaries of the Louisiana Purchase, where the Missouri Compromise had outlawed slavery. Scott now entered his third year on free soil.

At Fort Snelling, Scott married Harriet Robinson, a much younger slave girl, whom Emerson had bought. Dred and Harriet Scott remained married until his death twenty years later. Of their four children, two sons died in infancy. Two daughters, Eliza and Lizzie, became parties in their father's suit for freedom.

*Dred Scott and
his wife Harriet.*

Emerson, who complained of illness all of his life, did not remain at Fort Snelling for long. In 1837, he received a sick leave, and traveled down the Mississippi to St. Louis. But he left Scott and his wife at Fort Snelling, planning to send for them later. Then new orders arrived, and Emerson was sent to Fort Jesup in western Louisiana. There, in February 1838, he married Eliza Irene Sanford. After his marriage, Emerson needed more servants and sent for Dred and Harriet Scott to join him. In the spring of 1838, the Scotts journeyed by steamboat down the river to Louisiana, which brought them back into slaveholding territory.

By the fall, however, Emerson was on his way back to Fort Snelling, with his wife and the Scott family. From St. Louis, they began the 900-mile (1,440-kilometer) journey upriver to the Iowa Territory. On their trip upriver on a steamboat called the *Gypsy*, the Scott's first daughter Eliza was born—on the northern boundary of Missouri, in free territory. Then in the spring of 1840, Emerson was replaced as Fort Snelling's surgeon; once again, he was transferred South—this time to Florida. His wife remained in St. Louis, along with the Scotts.

In the fall of 1842, Emerson received an honorable discharge from the Army and returned to St. Louis. Shortly after, he moved with Mrs. Emerson back to the Iowa Territory. Harriet and Dred Scott remained in St. Louis. In December 1843, Emerson died.

Even though their master had died, Scott and his family remained slaves. Although there is some confusion among historians over the terms of Emerson's will, this is clear: Emerson left Dred Scott, his wife Harriet, and their daughter Eliza as slaves, under the ownership of his wife.

It was in the years following Emerson's death that Scott began to take the legal steps toward freedom that would eventually lead to the Supreme Court.

3

The Missouri Lawsuits

According to a story he later gave to journalists, Dred Scott tried to buy his own and his wife's freedom from Mrs. Emerson, but she refused. So on April 6, 1846, with the advice and backing of the Blow family and lawyers, Dred and Harriet Scott filed petitions in the Missouri circuit court in St. Louis to request permission to sue Mrs. Emerson for their freedom.

The petitions described how they had lived with Emerson on free soil. This would form the basis of their claims to freedom. The judge granted permission without hesitation, and on that very same day, Dred and Harriet Scott filed their first lawsuits.

Under Missouri slave law, a person was required to sue for his or her freedom by suing for damages. Yet under the law, assault and imprisonment were considered lawful punishment of a *slave*. Therefore, the jury first had to decide whether the plaintiff (the person who sues) was a slave, before deciding whether he or she had been mistreated. If the Scotts were free, it was illegal to beat and imprison them. If they were slaves, it was not.

In his suit, Dred Scott charged Mrs. Emerson with assault and false imprisonment: She had "beat, bruised, and ill-treated him" then imprisoned him for twelve hours. He also declared that he was a "free person" held in slavery, and sought $10 in damages. In this way, Dred Scott began two distinct suits against Mrs. Emerson. Harriet's suits against Mrs. Emerson were the same.

After many delays, the case was finally argued in June 1847, in the still uncompleted courthouse in St. Louis, now known as the "Old Courthouse." The presiding judge was a newcomer named Alexander Hamilton, from Philadelphia. The attorney speaking for Scott was probably Samuel Mansfield Bay, a former attorney general of Missouri. Mrs. Emerson was represented by George W. Goode, a pro-slavery resident of St. Louis who came from Virginia.

The Scotts' lawyers knew that the highest court of the state had already ruled in a number of similar cases in favor of former slaves. They had agreed that masters who took their slaves to live in free territory thereby set them free. All the Scotts' lawyers had to do was prove that Dred and Harriet Scott had lived in free territory and that Mrs. Emerson treated them as slaves.

The first part was easy to prove. Witnesses stated they had known Scott and his wife at Fort Armstrong and Fort Snelling. But, to everyone's surprise, trouble arose when they tried to prove the second part—that Mrs. Emerson used them as slaves. The chief witness for the Scotts was a man named Samuel Russell. He had hired the Scotts from Mrs. Emerson, paying the money to her father, Colonel Alexander Sanford. Such an arrangement would have meant that Mrs. Emerson treated the Scotts as slaves.

But when cross-examined by Lawyer Goode, Russell made a startling admission. His wife—not he—had made the arrangements to hire the Scotts. In fact, he knew nothing about it, except what his wife had told him, and all he did was pay the money to Colonel Sanford.

Russell's testimony sank the Scotts' case. Everyone knew they were Mrs. Emerson's slaves. But none of the testimony absolutely proved this to be so. It was enough of a weakness in the Scotts' case for the jury to decide in favor of Mrs. Emerson.

Immediately after they lost, on July 1, 1847, the Scotts' lawyers asked for a retrial, arguing that Russell's testimony had caught them off guard. At the same time, the Scotts each petitioned to file a new pair of suits against Alexander Sanford, Samuel Russell, and Irene Emerson. These were the three people who were closest to holding the Scotts as slaves, and this was a way for the Scotts to close the legal loophole that had given them so much trouble.

But within a month, Judge Hamilton ordered the Scotts to choose between their pair of lawsuits—against Mrs. Emerson or Sanford, Russell, and Emerson. The Scotts decided to sue Mrs. Emerson.

———

For the next three years, before the case came to trial, it became increasingly clear that neither side would give up easily. Mrs. Emerson seemed determined to keep possession of her slaves. At the same time, the Scotts were determined to make themselves free.

On January 12, 1850, the second trial of *Scott* v. *Emerson* came before Judge Hamilton in the St. Louis courthouse. By now, each side had new lawyers. Alexander P. Field, a famous trial lawyer and politician from Illinois, argued for the Scotts. On the other side was Hugh A. Garland, a former professor of Greek and a legislator from Virginia.

Dred Scott's trial was held before Harriet's. This time, Mrs. Russell testified that the Scotts were, indeed, hired as slaves. Mrs. Emerson's lawyers countered that military forts did not count as free territory, so that when Dred Scott lived in Fort Armstrong and Fort Snelling he was not on free soil. But at the end of the trial, when Judge Hamilton directed the jury to make their decision, it became clear that the judge favored Scott. The jury agreed. They ruled that Dred Scott should be free but made no ruling on Harriet's case.

It was not over. The lawyers and family members behind Mrs. Emerson were not ready to give up. And by 1852, when their appeal was finally ruled on, the political climate had changed.

4

Swept Up in the Conflict

*I*n the years* during which Dred Scott's case moved slowly through the Missouri courts the nation was becoming unhinged over slavery. A month after Scott brought his first suit against Mrs. Emerson, the United States went to war with Mexico over the southern border of Texas, which had just joined the Union. Southerners rallied behind the Mexican War, but Northerners believed it was part of a plan to extend slavery in the Southwest. On August 8, 1846, David Wilmot, a Democratic congressman from Pennsylvania, proposed his famous Proviso, which would have prohibited slavery from any land that might be acquired as a result of the battle.

Slavery had been a central political issue since the 1830s, when the United States began its rapid expansion across the West. But during the late 1840s, slavery was the central conflict in American political and social life.

With the end of the Mexican War in 1848, the United States acquired huge tracts of land, including New Mexico and California, where thousands upon thousands of prospectors were rushing in search of gold. President Zachary Taylor's proposal that both be admitted as free states so infuriated Southerners that South Carolina threatened to secede, or withdraw, from the Union.

The congressional struggle that followed resulted in the Compromise of 1850. California would be admitted as a free state, while slavery in the new territories of New Mexico and Utah would be left up to the people who lived there. In addition, the North had to agree to one more thing. An act was passed that made it the responsibility of the federal government to return runaway slaves to the South and slavery. This was the Fugitive Slave Act, and it obviously resembled the fugitive slave clause in the Constitution.

Northerners reacted with outrage and fury. They were horrified at being forced to obey a law that went against their anti-slavery beliefs. And they were bitterly resentful of the extension of Southern power into their states. Abolitionists (people who wanted to abolish slavery) issued anti-slavery editorials, sermons, books, and resolutions, and they staged fugitive slave "rescues." They argued that it was everyone's moral duty to break this immoral law. Harriet Beecher Stowe wrote her fiery anti-slavery novel *Uncle Tom's Cabin* to protest against the Fugitive Slave Act.

Not surprisingly, Southerners responded in kind, hardening their position for slavery. And with slavery under attack, they were in no mood for lawsuits favoring freedom. When Mrs. Emerson's lawyers appealed the 1850 decision in favor of Scott and took *Scott v. Emerson* to the state supreme court, they succeeded in getting the decision they wanted. On March 22, 1852, a divided court reversed the lower court's decision to rule in favor of Mrs. Emerson.

The Fugitive Slave Act outraged many Northerners, who were put in the position of upholding a law they strongly disagreed with. This picture shows two slaves who were captured in Boston being escorted to the boat that would take them back to their masters in South Carolina.

Harriet Beecher Stowe became famous overnight once Uncle Tom's Cabin *was published. Abolitionists loved her, and pro-slavery forces in the South felt exactly the opposite. Many people believed that her book, because it was so widely read, urged the nation into the Civil War.*

The presiding state supreme court judge, William Scott, knew that he was going against precedent (something previously established). In 1837 a case similar to Scott's, *Rachel* v. *Walker,* had established the legal principle in Missouri of "once free, always free" for slaves. As Judge Scott put it: "Times are not now as they were when the former decisions on this subject were made. Since then not only individuals but States have been possessed of a dark and fell spirit in relation to slavery. . . . Under such circumstances it does not behoove the State of Missouri" to do anything that might strengthen this anti-slavery spirit.

The Dred Scott case had been swept up in the national conflict over slavery.

THE CASE OF MARGARET GARNER

THE MOST SHOCKING fugitive slave case is that of Margaret Garner, who killed her own daughter to keep her from being returned to slavery. Garner, her husband Simon, and their four children were the slaves of Archibald K. Gaines, who owned a plantation in Kentucky. Late at night on January 27, 1856, the Garners fled with nine other slaves across the frozen Ohio River, into the free state of Ohio. Margaret Garner was pregnant at the time.

When they reached Cincinnati, the Garners hid in the house of their relative, Elijah Kite. Within hours, an arresting party surrounded the house, demanding the surrender of the fugitives, under the Fugitive Slave Act. Inside, the frightened slaves barred the doors and windows. Suddenly, Margaret Garner seized a butcher knife and cut the throat of her three-year-old daughter. Elijah Kite's wife grabbed the knife, while Garner sobbed that she would rather kill every one of her children than have them taken back across the river.

Three days later, hearings were begun in the federal courthouse to determine if Gaines could reclaim his slaves. Lawyers for the Garners stated that the Garners had been made free by their previous visits to Cincinnati, and so were free at the time of their flight. They also had the Garner adults arrested for murder, since they preferred to be hanged than sent back to slavery.

When it was over, the presiding judge ruled that the Garners be delivered up to the master and returned to slavery.

5

An Appeal to the Supreme Court

While their family's fate was being decided in the Missouri courts, Dred and Harriet Scott had been working for Charles Edmund La-Beaume, one of Peter Blow's sons-in-law. LaBeaume had hired them from Mrs. Emerson. Then, sometime after the April 1852 decision, Mrs. Emerson is thought to have sold the Scotts to John F. A. Sanford, her brother. Sanford, who lived in New York City, traveled often to St. Louis on business.

With a new owner, who was a resident of New York, the Scotts were entitled to bring a new lawsuit in the U.S. Supreme Court. This was because federal courts had the right to decide cases between citizens of different states.

Although the Scotts' personal desire for freedom was most likely the origin of *Dred Scott* v. *John F. A. Sanford*, the Supreme Court case that would absorb the nation, many people suspected that the lawsuit was really a political plot. Some thought that *Dred Scott* v. *Sanford* was created by abolitionists, who hoped to use the case to challenge slavery. Others saw the suit as a pro-slavery plan that would ultimately strengthen pro-slavery laws.

Before moving to the Supreme Court, *Dred Scott* v. *Sanford* had to pass through the United States circuit court for the district of Missouri. Scott's case was heard in 1854, in a small rented room over a Main Street store, where, because the court had no permanent home, the circuit court trials were held.

As before, Dred Scott stated that he was a citizen of Missouri who had been illegally assaulted and imprisoned, along with his family, by John Sanford. The damages sought this time were $9,000. Also as before, the verdict came in for the defendant. Scott was ruled to be Sanford's slave, and therefore Sanford had the right to treat him as he wished.

But this time, Dred Scott's case raised a new question with broader implications. Was Scott a citizen of Missouri? This was different from the question of whether he was a slave, for it touched upon a somewhat different matter: Could black people under *any circumstances* be considered citizens?

Sanford had challenged Scott's assertion that he was a citizen by arguing that because he was a black man descended from slaves of "pure African blood," he was not in fact a citizen of Missouri. But the presiding judge, Robert W. Wells, had ruled that for the purpose of filing a suit, citizenship meant simply residence in the state and the legal right to own property.

But this left a contradiction in the case. If Scott was a slave and had always been a slave, he was not a citizen of Missouri with the right to bring a lawsuit in the first place.

As soon as the trial ended, Scott's lawyer took steps to move the case to the Supreme Court. At this time, in 1854, not many people had heard of Dred Scott. Even so, the local St. Louis *Herald* covered the trial, concluding its report in this way: "Dred is, of course, poor and without any powerful friends. But no doubt he will find at the bar of the Supreme Court some able and generous advocate, who will do all he can to establish his right to go free."

Now Scott's supporters needed a prominent attorney to handle Scott's case in Washington. They published a twelve-page pamphlet, dated the Fourth of July for symbolic effect, which was said to be by Dred Scott himself. The pamphlet ended with the following appeal: "I have no money to pay anybody at Washington to speak for me. My fellow-men, can any of you help me in my day of trial? Will nobody speak for me at Washington, even without hope of other reward than the blessings of a poor black man and his family?"

The man who came forward was Montgomery Blair. Blair was forty-one, and had left St. Louis the year before to practice law in Washington. He had already established himself as an important player in the nation's capital. Tall and with a military bearing (he had been a West Point cadet), Blair was a strong supporter of the free-soil cause, even though he had once owned slaves and was not an advocate of anti-slavery causes. Sincere and intellectual, he was interested in literature and art as well as politics and law.

Meanwhile, the opposing side was marshalling its legal forces. Sanford's two lawyers were men of high reputation and standing in Washington. The first was the pro-slavery senator Henry S. Geyer from Missouri. Sanford's other lawyer, Reverdy Johnson of Maryland, was a former senator and attorney general under President Taylor. He was also one of the country's most respected constitutional lawyers and an old friend of Chief Justice Taney. Clearly, Dred Scott's case was important in pro-slavery circles.

Montgomery Blair agreed to argue Dred Scott's case in court. Reverdy Johnson, his legal opponent, was unfortunately an old friend of Chief Justice Taney.

The Supreme Court officially received *Scott* v. *Sanford* on December 30, 1854. But many cases from around the country were already waiting their turn to be heard. As a result, Dred Scott's case did not actually come before the Court until February 11, 1856. By then, a new slavery crisis had erupted in the nation and a bitter presidential election had begun. Slavery was tearing at the seams of the Union.

6

Violence and Turmoil

On February 11, 1856, the Supreme Court began to hear lawyers in the case of *Scott* v. *Sanford*. And newspapers began to note the potential significance of Dred Scott's case against Sanford. The Washington *Evening Star* observed that "the public of Washington do not seem to be aware that one of the most important cases ever brought up for adjudication by the Supreme Court is now being tried before that august tribunal." Editor Horace Greeley wrote in his New York *Tribune* that the court would soon decide "a most important case, involving the validity [in its day] of the Missouri restriction" of slavery in the territories.

Why were these newspapermen beginning to take notice? Because the issues at the center of Dred Scott's case—the rights of slaves brought to live on free soil and the status of African Americans as citizens—were tangled up with the conflict between the states and the federal government to regulate slavery.

In 1854, President Franklin Pierce had passed the Kansas-Nebraska Act, allowing for the residents of Kansas and Nebraska to decide for themselves whether they would be slave or free. Kansas, which bordered on slaveholding Missouri, was deeply divided on the issue. In 1855, just one year before Scott's case was heard, more than two hundred people were killed in Kansas, fighting over slavery. Abolitionists from New England, including John Brown, a well-known militant, poured into Kansas, hoping to gain control. At the same time, pro-slavery gangs moved in from Missouri to meet them. The struggle became known as "Bleeding Kansas."

A few months after the opening hearing of *Scott* v. *Sanford*, the nation was overwhelmed by a sensational event in the Senate. For seven days in May, Massachusetts senator Charles Sumner delivered a rousing speech against slaveholding. When South Carolina's young congressman Preston Brooks heard about the speech, he rushed onto the Senate floor and beat Sumner mercilessly with his cane. Sumner collapsed to the floor, bleeding heavily. It was three years before he recovered.

Soon, more bloodshed in Kansas agitated the nation. First, pro-slavery Kansans attacked free-soil settlers in Lawrence, Kansas. Then, on May 24, 1856, at Pottawatomie Creek in Kansas, John Brown and seven others rounded up five men whom they accused of the attack and killed them without a hearing or trial.

Slavery was also the key issue in the 1856 presidential election between James Buchanan and John C. Frémont. Buchanan wooed Southern Democrats by opposing interference in Southern affairs. Frémont, on the other hand, was the first presidential candidate of the new Republican party, which formed specifically to oppose slavery. His slogan was "Free Speech, Free Press, Free Soil, Free Men, Frémont, and Victory."

Against this background of violence and political turmoil, Dred Scott's case was brought before the Supreme Court.

SOUTHERN CHIVALRY — ARGUMENT VERSUS CLUB'S.

The attack upon Sumner by Brooks was reported in all the news magazines. The sarcastic caption would seem to indicate that this cartoon ran in a Northern publication.

7

"No Rights"

On February 11, 1856, Montgomery Blair entered the old courtroom in the basement of the Capitol to present his client's case to the nine Supreme Court judges. He had no taste for long-winded speeches or high drama, and he planned to argue the case precisely, accurately, and earnestly. On this day, he would argue Scott's case alone in his high-pitched voice and stiff manner. Sanford's lawyers, the cold Senator Geyer and the imposingly aristocratic Reverdy Johnson, would answer him.

The lengthy arguments of both sides took four days to deliver. Blair's arguments on Scott's behalf followed the course set in the circuit court: that Scott was a citizen and that living in free territory with his master meant that he had become free. Blair also made a special plea for Eliza, the older daughter, who had been born on a steamboat in free territory, north of the Missouri line.

Then, going further than Scott's earlier lawyers had, Blair argued for the constitutionality of the Missouri Compromise and the federal government's power to prohibit slavery in the western territories. Did not the elimination of the slave trade in the Constitution show that the Founding Fathers were against slavery?

When Geyer and Johnson answered Blair, they argued just as strongly that the Missouri Compromise was unconstitutional. Congress had no right to limit slavery in the West.

Thus, when the day's arguments had come to a close, Dred Scott's suit for freedom, as the newspapers realized, had become the critical political issue of the day.

In May 1856, the Supreme Court ordered that the case be reargued. They did not hear the rearguments until December 15. By then, it had become clear to the nine justices that they had a case of dynamite on their hands. Just two weeks earlier, President Pierce, in his final annual address to Congress, had declared the Missouri Compromise "a mere nullity . . . a monument of error . . . a dead letter in law." Republican senators reacted with outrage, and a furious debate followed. Whatever they decided, someone would explode.

On December 15, a large, eager audience filled the old courtroom to hear the lawyers in *Scott* v. *Sanford* argue about the Missouri Compromise and the rights of black citizenship. It was reported that many in the audience were distinguished judges and congressmen.

This time, Montgomery Blair was assisted by George T. Curtis, who was willing to present a defense for congressional power in the western territories. Neither of Scott's lawyers were known as anti-slavery men, even though they supported the Missouri Compromise. But both of Sanford's lawyers owed their careers to pro-slavery forces.

By the end of the year, Sanford had been stricken with a mental illness and was committed to an asylum. It was obvious that the defendant in the case was no longer Sanford but the slaveholding South. Late in the case, Reverdy Johnson would make this clear, when he declared that slavery would last "for all time."

For twelve hours, over the course of four days, Chief Justice Taney, along with the other eight justices, listened to the alternating arguments of the opposing lawyers. On December 18, Curtis concluded arguments for Scott, and the case was committed to the Court for its decision.

But the justices could not meet to discuss their views of the case until February 14. The wife of a justice had died on January 3, when her clothing caught fire, and he was too grief-stricken to return immediately to Washington.

Of the nine justices, five were from the South, including Chief Justice Taney. In the eyes of many observers, the makeup of the Court almost guaranteed that Scott would lose. But everyone knew that the arguments used in the decision would determine the political effects of the ruling.

Before announcing their decision, the nine justices were also subtly pressured by the president-elect, James Buchanan. Buchanan wanted to say something about the Missouri Compromise in his inaugural address in March, and he wanted to be sure that the Supreme Court was going to rule on this issue. By the end of February, Buchanan got what he wanted: a letter of assurance from one of the justices as to the case's "probable result."

Chief Justice Taney swore in the new president before a crowd assembled in front of the Capitol on March 4. For a few brief moments afterward, he and President Buchanan exchanged some whispered words. Then Buchanan turned to the throng and gave his address. In it, he declared that nothing could be "fairer than to leave the people of a Territory free" to decide for them-

THE PRESIDENTIAL CAMPAIGN OF '56.

In the presidential race between Buchanan and Frémont slavery
was a key issue. In this cartoon Buchanan is referring to slavery
as a "peculiar institution." In the old sense of the word, "peculiar"
meant that something was untouchable by any legal system.

selves about slavery before statehood. In other words, Buchanan announced a basically pro-slavery view on the territorial issue of slavery two days before Chief Justice Taney delivered the Court's views on the question.

On March 6, 1857, Justice Taney took up the papers on which his decision was written and began to read it before the packed audience, who were bristling with excitement. This was the moment they had all been waiting for. All eyes and ears were strained toward the aging chief justice.

Born almost eighty years earlier on his family's estate in Maryland, Roger Brooke Taney was the nation's fifth chief justice, since his confirmation in 1836. A man of some wealth, he had freed the slaves he had inherited. Still, he was no supporter of the anti-slavery movement.

In a feeble, weary voice, Taney read that the "unalienable rights" of "all men" affirmed in the Declaration of Independence did not apply to the descendants of African-born slaves. This was true, also, in the Constitution. In that document, Taney claimed, "Negroes" were not considered "as a portion of the people or citizens of the Government then formed." Dred Scott—as a black person —was not a citizen of the United States. Therefore, he was not entitled to sue in its courts.

The crowd drew its breath as the judge continued. Were Scott and his family free because they had lived in territory where slavery was forbidden by the Missouri Compromise? That depended, Taney reasoned, on whether Congress had the power to make such a ruling. But, he read on, those territories acquired after 1787 were not intended to be held as "colonies" under the control of the federal government. Congress's power over the western territories was, therefore, severely limited. As a result, Taney concluded, it

Chief Justice Roger Brooke Taney

was unlawful to deprive a citizen of his property, including his slave, in any part of the United States.

Two hours later, an exhausted Justice Taney stopped speaking. Then, each of the other justices took their turns delivering their opinions, including the two Northern anti-slavery judges who disagreed with the majority. But the decision that mattered was the majority ruling as given by Taney. And Taney had closed off completely Dred Scott's right to seek freedom through the courts. According to Taney, blacks "had no rights which the white man was bound to respect." Not only could slaves not sue, but *free* blacks could not sue, either.

8

Half Slave, Half Free

The Supreme Court decision on Dred Scott's case drew immediate reaction from all sides. Preachers delivered their views on the case in their Sunday sermons. State legislatures issued formal protests or formal praise. Newspapers took sides.

The New York *Tribune* dismissed the decision as having "just so much moral weight as would be the judgment of a majority of those congregated in any Washington bar-room." The five justices who decided against Scott, this correspondent wrote, were "the High Priests of Slavery." The Chicago *Tribune* called Taney's opinion "shocking to the sensibilities and aspirations of lovers of freedom and humanity."

On the other side, the Richmond *Enquirer* cheered that abolitionism had been "staggered and stunned" and that the "diabolical doctrines" of Northern fanatics had been struck down. The Charleston *Mercury* claimed that pro-slavery radicals had been "simply a step in advance" of the Supreme Court. In the middle, the Washington *Daily Union* called for calm. Pointing out that the "highest judicial authority" has decided "in accordance with the Constitution," they blamed professional troublemakers for stirring up trouble. "We have a race of agitators all over the country; their livelihood consists in agitating. . . ."

Politicians seeking office felt that they had to take a stand on the case. On June 26, 1857, an Illinois lawyer named Abraham Lincoln, who had just been nominated to run against Stephen A. Douglas for his seat in the Senate, gave a speech on the Dred Scott decision in Springfield. Lincoln called the Dred Scott decision "erroneous"—wrong. He believed that "colored persons" were citizens, in accord with the Constitution. They were "included in the body of 'the people of the United States.' " Later, in another speech, Lincoln referred to the Dred Scott decision and announced that "this government cannot endure, permanently half *slave* and half *free*."

In May 1858, Taylor Blow of St. Louis, a member of the family that had once owned Scott, bought Dred Scott and his family and quietly freed them. Over the next year, the Dred Scott decision was frequently brought up as part of an issue that was becoming increasingly clear: that slavery and freedom could not exist together much longer in the United States.

———

Dred Scott died on September 17, 1858. Little is known of his brief life in freedom. But the case that bears his name is important for several reasons. It raised the question of black civil rights in an age in which most white Americans considered African Americans to be inferior. Even Lincoln, though he believed in equality before the law, believed that black people were not inherently the equal of whites.

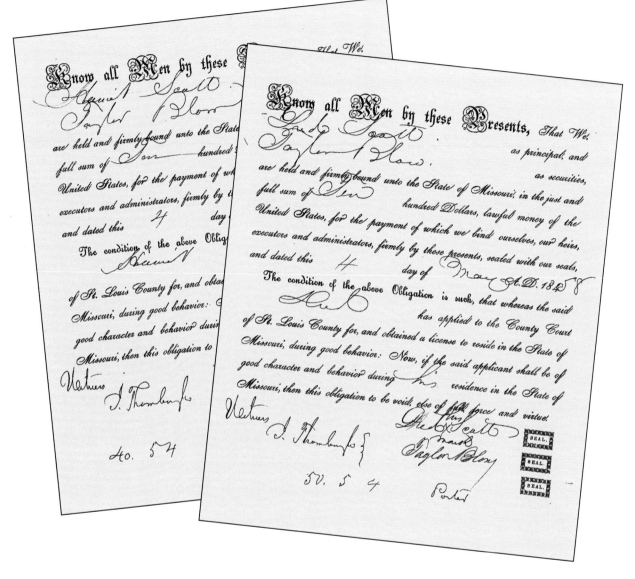

*These papers show that Dred and Harriet Scott were given
their freedom by Taylor Blow and, as of May 4th, 1858,
became residents in their own right of St. Louis, Missouri.*

The challenge to the constitutional treatment of black people in Dred Scott's case emerged in a series of amendments following the Civil War. In December 1865, Congress passed the Thirteenth Amendment to the Constitution to abolish slavery. "Neither slavery nor involuntary servitude . . . shall exist within the United States." The Fourteenth Amendment and civil-rights acts of 1866 and 1875 guaranteed African Americans unrestricted access to public places. The Fifteenth Amendment guaranteed the right to vote.

But Dred Scott's case also became a model for denying civil rights to African Americans. After Dred Scott, the most notorious example of the court's negation of black citizenship is the 1896 ruling in *Plessy* v. *Ferguson*, which legalized segregation in public places and made African Americans second-class citizens.

Another legacy of the Dred Scott case concerns the power of the Supreme Court to affect the law of the land. Critics of Taney's decision immediately claimed that the Court had gone too far. One newspaper editor complained that "from being the expounders [explainers] of law, [the Supreme Court justices] have become the makers of law." Today, legal scholars criticize Taney's decision as being an inappropriate use of the Court (meaning that the Court should not be able to decide matters for which there is no clear constitutional authority).

———

On May 11, 1857, in the midst of African-American despair following the Dred Scott ruling, the famous ex-slave orator Frederick Douglass spoke to the Anti-Slavery Society in New York. He affirmed his faith in the anti-slavery movement and America's progress toward justice. And he stated his belief in the integrity of the Constitution by citing its opening:

This painting by T. S. Noble is entitled The Last Sale of Slaves in Saint Louis. *It records a slave auction that took place in 1865 on the steps of the St. Louis courthouse where Dred Scott's case was first argued.*

"'We, the people,'" Douglass proclaimed, "not we, the white people—not we, the citizens, or the legal voters—not we, the privileged class, and excluding all other classes but we, the people; not we, the horses and cattle, but we, the people—the men and women, the human inhabitants of the United States, do ordain and establish this Constitution. . . ."

Chronology

1600s   Development of slavery and slave codes in British colonies.

1787   Signing of Constitution, which contained three clauses dealing with slavery.

1795   Dred Scott born in Virginia; called Sam.

1820   The Missouri Compromise, which banned slavery north of latitude 36°30'.

1830   Peter Blow family and slaves settle in St. Louis, Missouri.

1833   Dr. John Emerson takes his recently purchased slave, Dred Scott, to Fort Armstrong, Illinois.

1836   Dr. Emerson transferred to Fort Snelling, near what would become St. Paul, Minnesota. Dred Scott, therefore, enters third year of living on free soil.

        Dred Scott marries slave woman named Harriet Robinson, also owned by Emerson.

1838   Dred and Harriet journey down Mississippi River by steamboat to join Emerson and his new wife in western Louisiana.

1838–39 Scotts and Emersons take steamboat trip back to Iowa Territory. Scotts' first daughter, Eliza, born on the northern boundary of Missouri, in free territory.

1840–43 Scotts live in St. Louis for two years with Mrs. Emerson, remaining there after she moves to Iowa Territory with her husband, who soon dies. In his will, Emerson leaves Scotts to his wife.

1846   Scotts file first lawsuits for assault and unlawful imprisonment against Mrs. Emerson.

Mexican War and Wilmot Proviso, proposal to prohibit extension of slavery into the territories.

1847   Scotts' lawyers lose trial and petition Missouri courts for retrial.

1850   Second trial of *Scott* v. *Emerson* comes before Judge Hamilton in the St. Louis courthouse; decided in favor of Dred, but put off decision in Harriet's suit. Emerson's lawyers appeal decision.

Compromise of 1850, which includes Fugitive Slave Act.

1852   State Supreme Court reverses lower court's ruling and decides in favor of Mrs. Emerson. She probably sells Scotts to her brother, John F. A. Sanford. Scotts file new lawsuit.

1854   *Dred Scott* v. *Sanford* is heard in the United States circuit court for the district of Missouri. Decision again is against Scott. Montgomery Blair comes forward to take Scott's case to the Supreme Court. Supreme Court receives case on December 30.

1855   "Bleeding Kansas," where anti-slavery and pro-slavery forces clash.

1856   Supreme Court holds hearings in the case of *Scott* v. *Sanford*.

Anti-slavery senator Charles Sumner of Massachusetts beaten on Senate floor by South Carolina congressman.

John Brown massacre.

President James Buchanan elected.

1857   Chief Justice Roger Brooke Taney delivers Supreme Court decision on *Scott* v. *Sanford*, ruling against Scott.

1858   Dred Scott and Harriet are quietly given their freedom.

Further Reading

Connell, Kate. *Tales from the Underground Railroad*. Chatham, N.J.: Raintree Steck-Vaughn, 1992.

Rappaport, Doreen. *Escape from Slavery: Five Journeys to Freedom*. New York: HarperCollins Children's Books, 1991.

Shumate, Jane. *Sojourner Truth and the Voice of Freedom*. Brookfield, Conn.: Millbrook Press, 1991.

Smead, Howard. *The Afro-Americans*. New York: Chelsea House, 1989.

Stepto, Michelle, ed. *Our Song, Our Toil: The Story of American Slavery as Told by Slaves*. Brookfield, Conn.: Millbrook Press, 1994.

Bibliography

Fehrenbacher, Don E. *The Dred Scott Case: Its Significance in American Law and Politics.* New York: Oxford University Press, 1978.

Foner, Philip S., editor. *The Life and Writings of Frederick Douglass.* Vol. 2. New York: International Publishers, 1950.

Franklin, John Hope, and Alfred A. Moss, Jr. *From Slavery to Freedom: A History of Negro Americans.* Sixth Edition. New York: McGraw-Hill Publishing Co., 1988.

Hopkins, Vincent C. *Dred Scott's Case.* New York: Russell & Russell, 1967.

Lincoln, Abraham. *Speeches and Writings, 1832–1858.* New York: Library of America, 1989.

Stampp, Kenneth M. *America in 1857: A Nation on the Brink.* New York: Oxford University Press, 1990.

Sterling, Dorothy, ed. *We Are Your Sisters: Black Women in the Nineteenth Century.* New York: W. W. Norton & Co., 1984.

Index